BIRDS THAT HUNT

FOLLETT BEGINNING SCIENCE BOOKS

READING CONSULTANT
JEANNE S. BROUILLETTE
FORMERLY, CURRICULUM COORDINATOR
EVANSTON ELEMENTARY SCHOOLS

TECHNICAL CONSULTANT
AUSTIN L. RAND, Ph.D.
CHIEF CURATOR OF ZOOLOGY
FIELD MUSEUM OF NATURAL HISTORY

Birds that Hunt

BALD EAGLE

Willard Luce

ILLUSTRATED BY EDWIN HUFF

FOLLETT PUBLISHING COMPANY, CHICAGO

ISBN 0695-40799-6 Titan Edition

ISBN 0695-80799-4 Trade Edition

Library of Congress Catalog Card Number: 69-10263

First printing

Many birds live by hunting. They catch and eat rats, mice, and other small mammals. They also capture smaller birds, reptiles, fish, and insects. There are two large groups of them. One group, the owls, flies at night. The second group, with eagles, hawks and others, flies during the day.

Hunting birds are sometimes called birds of prey. They have sharp, curved claws, which are called talons, and hooked beaks used for tearing their food into small pieces. Birds of prey also have good eyesight. While flying high above the ground, a hawk can see a tiny mouse moving in the grass. A bald eagle can see prey that is two to three miles away.

BIRDS THAT HUNT HAVE SPECIAL BODY FEATURES

Their eyes are located more to the front of their head instead of being on the sides. They have a strong hooked beak that can tear meat. Most of them have powerful claws that can carry their prey. Some have wings for soaring and gliding, as well as for flapping flight.

Owls can fly without making any sound.

Many birds have eyes on the sides of their head.

Eagles and hawks can soar and glide.

Birds of prey have eyes more to the front.

Falcons fly by flapping and gliding.

Talons are long, sharp claws.

The Everglade kite uses its long hooked beak to take snails out of their shells.

The peregrine falcon's notched beak is used for killing its prey.

Talons are used to grasp and carry.

Talons are used to pierce and kill prey.

The beak of the California condor can cut and tear the heavy hide and tough muscles of dead animals.

Bald eagle nests usually are built in very tall trees or on cliffs. The young take three months to grow their feathers, learn to fly, and capture their own food.

Birds of the eagle and hawk family have powerful wings. They can fly fast and turn quickly. They are able to glide or soar on rising air currents. Hardly moving their wings, they can stay in the air for hours.

The female birds of this family are usually larger, stronger, and bolder than the males. Both parents usually take care of the eggs

It is against the law to kill a bald eagle. But every year many of them are shot. If this continues there will be no bald eagles left.

and, later, the young. They carry food in their talons back to the nest to feed to their young.

Many countries have chosen eagles as their national birds because eagles are so brave.

The bald eagle was chosen as the symbol of the United States. It is not really bald. It looks bald because its head feathers turn white when it is three years old.

The fierce golden eagle sometimes attacks animals too large to carry, especially if it is hungry.

The golden eagle is a powerful bird that once lived over much of the northern part of the earth. Now it is becoming rare. In many places, where the birds attack farm animals, golden eagles are hunted.

These eagles still live in western North America, Scotland, northern Europe, and the mountains of Asia.

The harpy eagle lives in the hot rain forest of South America. It is one of the largest birds of prey, measuring about 36 inches from beak to tail. A harpy can fly nearly straight up and down between the tall trees. It feeds on monkeys, sloths, opossums, and porcupines.

Some eagles will eat reptiles. Fourteen kinds of these birds live in Europe, Asia, and Africa. Reptile eaters have large heads that are covered with feathers. Some of these birds hunt and eat poisonous snakes.

The heavy feathers of the bataleur eagle of Africa protect it from the fangs of poisonous snakes.

The swallow-tailed kite of North and South America is one of the most graceful birds of prey.

Kites are rather small birds of prey with long, pointed wings. They are excellent fliers. Long ago in Europe they were protected as scavengers, because when garbage was thrown in the streets, kites came and ate it.

Now kites, like other birds of prey, are often shot by people who do not understand that the birds kill many rats and mice, as well as poisonous snakes.

Birds of the hawk family live all around the world. In North America, the Cooper's hawk and sharp-shinned hawk are known by the farmers for their chicken-stealing. These birds give the whole hawk family a bad name.

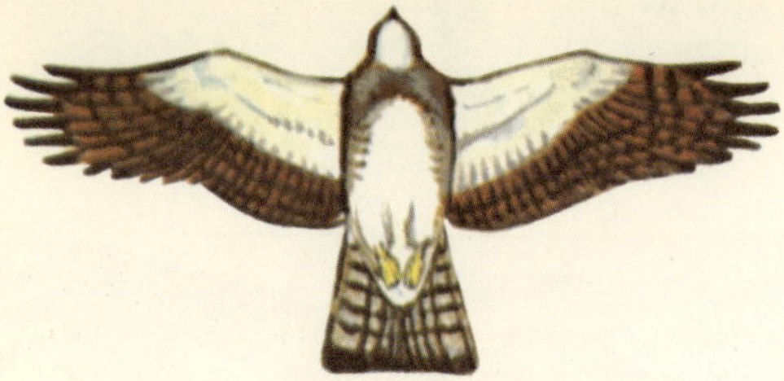

SWAINSON'S HAWK

RED-TAILED HAWK

BROAD-WINGED HAWK

RED-SHOULDERED HAWK

The red-tailed hawks and red-shouldered hawks have broad wings. They fly in wide circles high in the air. The broad-winged hawks, shown in the picture here, are very useful to man because they eat mice and rats.

The name, buzzard, is used for some hawks as well as for vultures.

Vultures are birds of prey that are useful in a different way. They have weak feet and cannot grasp and kill their prey. They eat things that are already dead. They help keep the outdoors clean.

The turkey vulture is often seen in parts of North and South America. They look ugly and clumsy on the ground, but in the air they are very graceful.

Both the California and South American condor have a wingspread of nine to eleven feet.

One kind of vulture, the condor, is one of the largest flying birds in the world. Most condors live in the high mountains and can soar for hours.

The California condor is very rare now. It lays only one egg about every two years and is easily scared from its nest. If this happens, the egg will not hatch. The South American condor is also scarce. But there are fewer men to bother it, so it is less likely to die out.

The osprey is a large bird of prey that can be found near water all over the world. It is sometimes called the fish hawk because it eats only fish. The osprey dives feet first into the water and grasps fish in its strong talons.

The osprey has a habit of hovering or floating above the water while searching for its food.

The sport of hunting with falcons is called falconry. This peregrine falcon is given a piece of meat as a reward for capturing a pheasant.

Falcons are the fastest birds of prey. They have long, pointed wings and a hooked beak. Falcons hunt in open country and prey mostly on other birds.

In Europe and Asia, men used to train falcons to hunt for them. The falcon owner wore a large glove, and the bird perched on the wrist. At a signal, the falcon flew after its prey and knocked it down. Then the falcon waited beside the prey until its owner arrived. Some people still hunt with falcons.

The sparrow hawk is also called the windhover because of the way it seems to float or hover in one spot over the fields.

Different falcons live all over the world. Best known in North America are the peregrine falcon or duck hawk, and the American kestrel or sparrow hawk.

The sparrow hawk is only about the size of a robin. Although it prefers insects as food, it can be trained to catch prey for a human master.

Owls are birds of prey that start hunting at night when the birds of the hawk family are sleeping. A few kinds of owls hunt in daylight, however. Owls are not related to hawks and eagles.

The large eyes of owls are made for seeing in the dark. These birds also have good hearing. An owl can catch a mouse it cannot even see. It follows the little animal by the sound of its movements.

Owls can turn their heads all the way around to see what is going on in back of them.

BARN OWL

SCREECH OWL

BARRED OWL

GREAT HORNED OWL

Owls have soft feathers. They can fly without making a sound. The birds twist and turn between trees and drop down to the earth before their prey knows they are near.

Sometimes owls scream. This frightens any animal that is near. As the animal races for a hiding place, the owl swoops down and catches it.

GREAT HORNED OWL

The great horned owl is one of the largest, measuring up to three feet from head to tail.

Owls eat mostly mice and other small animals. A single pair of owls will kill hundreds of harmful mice, gophers, and rats.

Great horned owls sometimes become fond of chicken meat. They can do great damage to farmers' flocks. But owls do far more good than harm, and they deserve to be protected.

Barn owls like to live in old buildings. Sometimes they find good hunting in large cities.

Many owls nest early in the year. Since it is still cold, the mother starts sitting on the nest as soon as the first egg is laid. The baby owls or owlets hatch at different times. The older ones get the most and the best food.

Screech owls may be grey or reddish-brown in color.

The large snowy owl only comes south when food is scarce in the Arctic regions.

The beautiful snowy owl lives in the arctic parts of the world. It is white with a few black markings. Because of its color, it is hard to see against the snow-covered ground.

The sun does not set for many days in the arctic summer. And so the snowy owl must be able to see and hunt in daylight. It eats ducks, lemmings, foxes, and hares.

SNOWY OWL

GREAT GREY OWL

LONG-EARED OWL

SHORT-EARED OWL

The hawk owl lives in the northern forests of Europe and America. It lives much like other owls, except that it hunts by day instead of by night. It will fight fiercely to protect its young from man or other enemies.

HAWK OWL

Burrowing owls nest in holes in the ground. Sometimes they dig these holes by themselves. But they may also move into a hole dug by another animal. These owls capture desert mice, lizards, and insects.

Elf owls are the smallest owls. They are no larger than sparrows and eat mostly insects. Elf owls make their homes in holes of cactus plants and trees.

Elf owls nest in holes that have been pecked out by desert woodpeckers.

Burrowing owls live peacefully with prairie dogs.

A pygmy owl will capture ground squirrels twice its own size.

Birds of prey are called "good" if they eat things which harm man. They are called "bad" if they eat animals which man wants for himself.

Some birds of prey that are called "bad" take only a few chickens. They really help farmers by eating mice and other rodents.

Birds of prey do kill game birds such as ducks, quail, and pheasants. Many scientists believe this is good. Game birds should be quick, alert, and hard to catch. Hawks, eagles, and owls can catch only the game birds that are sick, old, or weak. This leaves the strongest game birds to mate and raise young.

Birds of prey have a useful place in nature. They deserve to be protected.

Words Younger Children May Need Help With

(Numbers refer to page on which the word first appears)

4 mammals
reptiles
5 talons
prey
6 soaring
falcon
powerful
7 condor
peregrine
8 female
males
9 national
symbol
10 attack
11 harpy
sloths
opossums
porcupines
12 poisonous
13 scavengers
14 sharp-shinned
15 red-tailed
red-shouldered
broad-winged
buzzard
vultures
16 clumsy
17 scarce
18 osprey
19 falconry
20 kestrel
23 gophers
24 owlets
25 arctic
lemmings
28 burrowing
lizards
cactus
29 pygmy
30 pheasants
quail
scientists

Things to Do in the Classroom or at Home

Visit the bird house in a zoo.

Many zoos have large separate houses for their collection of living birds. Make a list of the birds of prey in this book. Take it to the zoo and see how many living specimens of birds you can see.

Enjoy some excellent bird photographs.

Check out a copy of *Hawks In Hand* by F. and L. Craighead from your library. This book has many fine photographs of hawks and falcons that were raised by the authors. Try to locate the January and February, 1970 issues of the National Wildlife Magazine. These issues feature articles on owls and hawks with excellent pictures.

Read an interesting story about a bird of prey.

You will enjoy reading either of these books: *Vulcan: the Story of a Bald Eagle* by R. McClung, Morrow, 1955, or *Otus: the Story of a Screech Owl* by L. Sandford, Morrow, 1959. One of your parents or your teacher will help you get them from the library.

Write a report on Hawk Mountain Sanctuary.

Write for literature about this unusual hawk sanctuary. Address your request to Hawk Mountain Sanctuary, Route 2, Kempton, Pennsylvania, 19529. See if your library has a copy of *Hawks Aloft* by Maurice Brown.